To our darling Matilda

Happy Christ

All our love

Nanny and Grandad.

x x x

x x

x

INSPIRING STORIES for AMAZING KIDS

A Motivational Book full of Magic and Adventures about Courage, Self-Confidence and the importance of believing in your dreams.

Nadia Ross

Special Art Stories

Inspirational Stories for Amazing Kids

A Motivational Book full of Magic and Adventures about Courage, Self-Confidence and the importance of believing in your dreams.

Nadia Ross

HARDCOVER ISBN: 9791255530916
support@specialartbooks.com
www.specialartbooks.com

Table of Contents

Introduction 4
Tommy & His Flying Sailboat 5
Hanna & Her Fairy 16
Erick Doesn't Want to Play 26
Baxley Gets the Job Done 35
The Mermaid Life 44
Sidnee and Her Problem 59
Danielle and Daniel 70
Vinny the Volcano 79
Little Joe the Elf Wants to Be a Wizard 89
Liam Wants an Adventure 96
Epilogue 107

Introduction

Hello! I am so happy you are here.

Each one of these stories is filled with an incredible message for you, my reader. Even though the characters come from a place that doesn't exist, you are going to understand what they go through because they face the same emotions, ideas, dreams, and desires that you feel every day.

And so, my amazing reader, you can reach into the lives of these fairy tales and see how the heroes of the stories overcome their challenges. When you do, think about how they came about accomplishing their goals and reaching their dreams.

Remember to take these stories into your heart and mind and keep them with you when you encounter similar problems, issues, or adventures. Even when things get tough, you can behave and act as your heroes do. You are the main character in your story.

Tommy & His Flying Sailboat

There are times when your ideas seem far too big to accomplish. These ideas are usually called DREAMS. Not the dreams you visit when you sleep. The dreams that come to you through hard work, dedication, and perseverance. These dreams can be turned into reality, even if they seem impossible.

Don't give up even when your dream seems unreachable. Take a step back and look at it differently. Then, you'll be able to find an answer to your problem and keep moving forward toward your goal.

When you do this, you'll be able to turn your dream into reality, and that will make your life a happy one.

~ ~ ~

Tommy lives in a city, similar to yours and mine, but his city is full of magic and floats over the sea on a cloud. To us, his city seems like every other cloud in the sky, but there are hundreds of towns like his. They have roadways that connect them, but instead of driving cars, they fly ships through the air.

In Tommy's city, the flowers look like jewels, their petals are gemstones, and they get watered with crystal plant food. These flowers are the colors of the deepest sea, the reddest ruby, and the greenest grass—all sparkle with magic and hum the special songs of bells.

Since they live in the clouds, they don't have bad weather. A warm breeze is blowing all the time, and they only use water to grow food, drink, and clean. Everyone walks in sandals that cushion their feet. They get to take the softest steps you've ever felt. They wear cloth pants in pastel colors and jackets that break the wind as it flows around the city buildings.

Their buildings and houses are made from bricks of greens, pinks, whites, and blues. They reach a magical warmth when the sun hits them just right, and they cool down if it becomes too hot.

Tommy loves his city, and when he walks through the streets, he knows how lucky he is. He adores in the beautiful buildings, trees, and plants. He loves the people and their kindness. But even though Tommy enjoys life in his magical cloud city, he knows that the world is big, and he longs for adventure.

The wind blows through his hair as he sits on the bow of his father's boat. They were going to pick up some fresh supplies from another city in the clouds, but all Tommy could do was look down at the flat-land. The land beneath the clouds is a patchwork of greens, browns, and tans. Tommy imagined what it would feel like to touch the grass with his bare feet and run his hand over a tree that grows on the land.

He knows there is an adventure down on the ground and has many dreams about exploring the green and blue parts of the world below. One day, Tommy sat back up and turned to his father. He said, "One day, I will sail my boat down to earth to see what I can find!"

Tommy's dad smiled at him and gave him a thumbs up. However, his dad was very realistic, and so he said, "You don't have a boat, Tommy. You'll have to wait until you get older!"

Tommy rolled his eyes. He was tired of waiting to get older. He got an idea as he looked over the horizon. He saw mountains carving zig-zagged lines in the sky and clouds that rolled by.

He would make his own boat.

Excitement mounted inside his belly as he started to list all the items he would have to get to make a boat. He'd helped his dad build the ship they were flying right now, so he knew that they needed certain boat parts like a bow and a wheel, but everything would be made of wood. Then, he would need a sail.

Special propellers would be cut in a certain way to push the boat over the air, and then the lastly ship would need wings.

Tommy let out a long sigh. That seemed like a lot of stuff to do. But he knew that if he made a smaller flying boat, it might not be too bad.

However, Tommy also knew that he couldn't do this project alone. He thought about asking his older brother to help him but considered that his dad would probably know more about flying boats since he had built a few already. He turned around with a wide smile toward his dad, "Can you help me build a boat now?"

His dad blinked in surprise because he wasn't expecting Tommy to be so dedicated to exploring that he wanted to craft a boat, but he didn't want to discourage his son either. Tommy's dad said, "Yes. But you cannot fly without a parent or grownup with you once we built the boat."

Tommy nodded in agreement. He could live with that.

After they got home from the market on the other cloud city, Tommy sat down and made a list of all his needed items. His dad helped him figure out how much he would have to get—by way of chopping down trees—and how much fabric he would need for the sail. Once they were done with the list, Tommy whistled. He didn't know where to start. He looked at his dad and said, "What should I do first?"

"Well, you can't build a boat without a frame. Gather the wood up over the next few days, and then we can get the wood ready to build the frame. Then, you'll have to get the fancy feathers from the tip-tall mountain bird to help your boat fly. And finally, you'll have to go to the big diamond mine to get the propeller cut in just the right way. Once you're done with that, you can worry about the paint and the sail. Those three tasks are the big ones. Plus, remember, you have school, and all schoolwork has to be done first."

There were three tasks he had to tackle. The first would be to cut down four tall fir trees. Cutting down the trees (and planting new ones in their place) took four days, one tree each day. Thankfully, Tommy's dad helped him bring the tall trees home. Tommy and his dad would spend four more days shaving off the cloud bark, branches, and leaves. By the end of one month, Tommy had all the wood he would need for his boat.

The next task he had to go on was to go up to Tip-Top Mountain and get special feathers from a CooCoo bird. Tommy went after school one day with a few friends. CooCoo birds were very friendly and gave their feathers to the people in the clouds. All they had to do was tell a story or sing a song. Tommy and his friends had come up with a great story about a dragon, a group of knights, and a bowling tournament. It was a funny story that Tommy and his friends enjoyed telling together.

One of Tommy's more courageous friends walked up to a CooCoo bird and said, "Excuse me. Would you like to hear a story in exchange for some feathers?"

The bird shook itself out and opened its long, burgundy beak to say, "Yes! I love stories!"

The boys acted out the story for the bird, and soon many other birds were paying attention. Once they were done with the story—the dragon at the bowling tournament—Tommy noticed that they had almost twenty CooCoo birds paying attention to them. He was ecstatic.

Several birds enjoyed the story so much that Tommy and his friends left with a full bag of feathers.

Tommy's final task was to go to the diamond mine. Since Tommy was a child, he would have to go with his dad. There were safety rules they had to follow, and children weren't allowed at the mine without a grownup.

When Tommy and his dad got to the mine, they took the propellers they had built from the wood and asked the diamond gnomes to help them cut the propellers so Tommy's boat would fly.

The gnomes looked at the propellers and nodded. They would cut them at just the right angle so the boat would fly smoothly. Tommy, in payment, pulled out sticky buns to give to the gnomes because diamond gnomes loved sweet desserts more than anything else.

It took a few days to get the propellers cut right, but while they were waiting for the final pieces, Tommy and his dad built the boat, placed the wings on it, and asked his mom if she could sew the sail, which she did gladly.

At last, the propellers were complete.

Tommy and his dad installed them into the bottom of the boat as his mom attached the sail to the mast.

Tommy was very excited. He was ready to fly down to the flatlands.

A few days later, Tommy and his dad were standing on the deck of his flying boat. The wings flapped in the breeze, ready to take off.

Tommy looked back at his mom, brother, and friends and waved. He gave his mom a thumbs up, and she untied the boat from the air dock.

The wind twisted through Tommy's hair as his boat slowly rose away from the cloud city. Tommy's dad placed a hand on his son's shoulder as he said, "I'm really glad you didn't give up."

Tommy looked at his dad with pride blooming in his chest and ready to leap out of his skin he excitedly said, "Me too, Dad. Let's go to land!"

And they took off on Tommy's first adventure.

~ ~ ~

Remember, hard work, dedication, and never giving up will always pay off. To get results, you have to take risks even when the stakes are scary. Even if you come across struggles or challenges, believing in yourself is the best way to turn your dreams into reality.

Always believe in your dreams. Have the courage to try your hardest, and always look for a new answer if you come up against a problem. You'll find the way to reach your goals, and it will be amazing.

Hanna & Her Fairy

Sometimes, we get so busy that we forget that other people are in the world, but other people will always be around no matter what you are doing or how you are feeling. There are moments when your eyes will open, and you'll realize how amazing it is to help someone in need.

Even if they are different from you.

Even if there is magic involved.

Even if you are a prince or princess.

No matter who you are in life, someone can always use your help. You don't have to use magic to do it, but magic sure does help in this story!

~ ~ ~

Princess Hanna and Prince Henry were twins who lived in a magical land where there were many different kinds of creatures. Trees spoke and talked to birds; witches would brew extraordinary potions that could heal broken bones or take the sickness out of someone who had started catching a cold. Frogs would sing their tadpoles to sleep at night with the most enchanting lullabies.

As kind and gentle as Hanna was, Henry was naughty and rowdy. He had a lot of energy that he liked to burn through on a day-to-day basis. He got angry quickly and had fits of rage when things didn't go his way.

However, Hanna wasn't afraid of her brother. Instead, she saw that he had strong emotions but wasn't sure how to channel them positively.

Because of Hanna's affection for her brother, she would often take him with her to play, although when his group of friends showed up, she would leave Henry with them as their aggressive behavior tended to be too much for her.

Hanna knew that Henry surrounded himself with friends who reflected how he felt about himself. He was angry. They were angry, although she wasn't sure why any of them were—she wasn't comfortable being around the group when they were loud and unruly.

One day, Hanna and Henry were walking through the forest when she heard a teeny, tiny noise that sounded like crying. Hanna put her hand on Henry's arm and said, "Do you hear that?"

Henry raised his eyebrow and looked at her like she was crazy, "No," he responded in a bored voice.

Instead of being swayed, Hanna got down on her hands and knees and tilted her ear to the long grass to see if she could find where the sound was coming from.

But Henry's friends weren't far behind them, and their shouts and whoops were soon upon the twins. Their commotion made it hard for Hanna to hear anything. She stood up with her arms crossed over her chest and said, "I cannot hear anything. I'm trying to find whatever or whoever is making a noise I heard, and your noisy clamor isn't helping me."

Knowing that Hanna was their princess didn't stop these boys from laughing at her. And Henry saw their reaction and joined in their merriment. Although he didn't feel comfortable making fun of his sister, he often felt as though she was too kind for her own good.

"Hanna, whatever is making a noise isn't worth your time," Henry said, "you are a princess. You need to act like one. You should only give your attention to things that are your equal."

Hanna looked to her brother, "Just because we rule over the land and all its beings it doesn't mean that we are any better than anything else. We are all equal here."

Henry rolled his eyes and said, "Come on, guys—let's leave Hanna to find whatever little bird has hurt itself."

As they walked away, Hanna shook her head at her brother's behavior and hoped that he really didn't believe he was better than other people, but a wiggly feeling in her belly told her that he did—for now, at least.

She let that worry go away and listened again for the tiny cries. As soon as she focused on the sound, she heard it. Hanna tilted her head again and parted long blades of the emerald green grass to find a fairy sitting on the ground with her head in her hands. The fairy's shoulders shook as though she was crying, and while it was hard for Hanna to hear her sobs, she could see that the creature was in distress.

Hanna did not want to scare the fairy, so she rustled the grass and whispered, "Hello?" to her. She knew that her voice, at a normal level, might sound like yelling to the fairy, and Hanna wanted to be as kind to her as possible.

The fairy looked up; her large purple eyes shone with tears but she wasn't startled. The fairy sniffled, "Hello, Princess."

Hanna gave a soft smile, "You seem so sad. What is your name? Is there anything I can do to help you?"

The fairy wiped her tears away and rubbed her eyes with her fists. She looked up at Hanna with drier eyes, even though they were a bit red. "I am Merryweather. I broke my wing and cannot fly."

Hanna looked at Merryweather's wing and saw that it was, in fact, bent in an awkward position. "Oh, my!" Hanna proclaimed, "Does it hurt badly?"

Merryweather shook her head and said, "I cannot fly if I broke my wing."

"Surely this has happened to fairies before. Do you know what they have done to fix it?"

Merryweather shook her head no again and then started to cry all over again.

Hanna bent over and said, "It's okay. Do you mind if I pick you up? I can help you, and we can find out how to fix your wing. I promise."

Merryweather blinked her big eyes at the Princess and tried to smile. She was grateful that Hanna was willing to help her but wasn't sure if it would work. Merryweather gave a quick nod of permission and said, "Yes. I will accept your help." The fairy knew that it wasn't every day a member of the royal family would offer their assistance to a fairy, and Merryweather also knew that Princess Hanna was special indeed.

Hanna took Merryweather to the castle, and they immediately looked for Hanna's grandmother, who used to be queen once but stepped down to let her children rule the land. Hanna's grandmother was excellent with healing. She learned a lot from witches in the hopes of helping out others.

When Hanna's grandmother, Grace, saw Merryweather's wing, she knew just what to do.

"Thank you for bringing her to me, Hanna," Grace said, "I think it's incredible that you want to help out everyone you can." Grandmother turned to look at the fairy. Her warm blue eyes crinkled with kindness and care; she said, "It will take a few weeks to heal your wing completely, Miss Merryweather. Are you okay staying in my granddaughter's room so we can watch after you?"

Merryweather's heart filled with love. "Thank you," she said. She was relieved that her wing would be healed and that she could fly again. She was also touched by how kind both royal family members were.

When Merryweather's wing was healing, Henry would come into Hanna's room from time to time. He would eye the small fairy in his sister's room and say things like, "I don't know why you are bothering to help this creature out," and "Don't we have people to do that?"

Hanna frowned at her brother to say, "You know she can understand you, right? Everything in our kingdom is ours to take care of."

Hanna knew that whenever she took care of something or someone, she showed all living creatures respect. She wanted to continue that no matter how much Henry told her that what she was doing was weird or wrong.

After a few weeks, Merryweather's wing was healed. Hanna was sad to see Merryweather leave but was excited to know that she had made a new friend. Plus, her grandmother had also begun teaching Hanna some healing tonics to help others who may become sick. Hanna always appreciated learning things.

When Merryweather went flying off, Henry was there. He said, "Now, I understand why. It's awesome to see your fairy friend flying off!"

Hanna smiled and was very happy that she had helped her brother learn something new. Anytime anyone or anything in the kingdom needed help both Hanna and Henry were there to help them.

~ ~ ~

We are all created equal, and treating everyone and everything with kindness is an amazing way to show all living creatures how much you care.

Erick Doesn't Want to Play

We all have times when something bothers us. Talking about your feelings and thoughts is the best way to get them out of your mind and heart.

It can also help you realize that maybe things aren't so bad.

But what happens when the words and feelings get too hard to say? Maybe your anger or fear seems far too big, and you don't want to share it with the world.

~ ~ ~

Erick lived with his dad and three brothers in their cottage. It was nestled behind some trees that were perfect for shading on hot days. Erick's brothers were rough and loud, but Erick enjoyed the quieter things in life. He liked to read, explore, and play with animals. Although the animals enjoyed wrestling around a little, they were much smaller and quieter than Erick's brothers. The animals in Erick's forest are very special; they talked and laughed and even went to school with him!

His best friend was a beaver whose name is Tod.

Tod and Erick had a lot of adventures. They explored caves and examined all sorts of items they have found. Erick and Tod even have a special cave where they hide their most secret treasures.

One day, when Erick was particularly grumpy, he told his father he wanted to go out and walked toward the door. Erick paused with his hand hovering over the golden knob before he heard his dad allow him to leave. As soon as he heard his dad say, "Be back by lunch," Erick was gone into the woods.

A little while later, Tod realized that he couldn't find his friend and grew worried. Erick's other animal friends, led by Tod, also became concerned.

Tod thought their animal crew was a great-looking bunch of creatures and beasts. There was Tod the Beaver, Alice the Bear, and Jane the Squirrel.

They looked at each other and said, "What should we do?" They never went on adventures without Erick, so Tod led the crew to Erick's cottage. They went to his window, which was how they usually invited him out to play, but the window was closed tight.

Tod said, "Maybe we should knock on the front door?"

The other animals agreed. Although they had never spoken with Erick's dad or brothers before, they knew they could talk to everyone in this forest. So, they walked to the front door, and Alice the Bear knocked as loudly as she could, which was pretty loud because she was a bear!

Soon after the knock, the door opened and a tall man who looked like Erick—only older—stood there looking down at the three animals. The animal crew could see a smile break through his red beard, and his brown eyes twinkled with kindness, "Hello? Are you looking for Erick?"

Tod straightened his shoulders, lifted his chin, and cleared his throat. He said, "Yes, sir. We are."

Erick's dad explained to Tod, Alice, and Jane that Erick had left earlier in the morning, "I'm not sure where he went, but I think Erick was in a bad mood. He really needs his friends. Can you find him and try to cheer him up?"

The animals looked at each other and knew what they wanted to do. They were going to find Erick!

"We will find him and help him out of the bad mood," Jane the Squirrel said.

"Wonderful," Erick's dad replied, "I am sure that you'll find Erick quickly. Please let me know as soon as possible!"

Tod, Jane, and Alice walked through the forest, looking for Erick under forts made from branches, behind trees, and around rocks. But they could not find Erick anywhere.

Just when they were going to give up hope, Tod remembered their secret cave. He turned to Alice and Jane and said, "I will show you someplace secret, but you cannot tell anyone about it."

The bear and the squirrel crossed their hearts and held up their hands. They promised neither would tell anyone unless they all agreed to invite someone in.

Tod led Jane and Alice on the secret path toward his cave. They climbed up a tree and stepped off a branch onto a ledge hidden from the ground. They hurried across the ledge and then found stairs made from stone.

The group then climbed those stairs and came right up to the mouth of a cave.

Jane and Alice were surprised to see the cave but excited to find something new.

"How did you ever find this place," asked Jane.

"Erick and I find all kinds of cool things in the forest. We are adventurers." Tod smiled at his friends, "I guess you guys are now too!"

The others smiled at each other and walked into the cave. They saw Erick sitting on the ground with his head in his hands.

The friends heard nothing for a few moments, and then they heard, "Go away, I don't want to talk."

"Erick," Jane said, "It's Jane, Alice, and Tod. We just want to talk to you."

Erick lifted his head. A look of surprise was on his face. He looked at Tod and said, "You invited our friends here? They promised not to share the secret?"

Tod cleared his throat and said, "Yes. We got worried when we didn't see you today. We want to talk."

"We want to see you even when you are grumpy," Alice said. "We like being with you just the way you are."

This statement surprised Erick, "But I'm grumpy today."

"Why?" Asked Tod.

"I woke up, and I was grumpy," Erick said.

"Sometimes, I wake up grumpy too," Alice said.

Erick looked up, surprised, "You do?"

Alice nodded and smiled. Her bear paws wrapped around herself, "But then because I'm sleepy, I drop things or hurt myself by accident. It makes the day feel much worse."

Erick nodded, now a little more enthusiastically, "That's what happened to me! I didn't sleep well last night. Then, I dropped my breakfast all over the floor today, spilled my milk, and stubbed my toe on the corner of my dresser!"

Erick was surprised to learn that this had also happened to his friend. As soon as he talked about his morning, he realized his sadness about his mistakes started to lift off of his chest, and instead, he began to feel relieved.

"Wow!" Erick said, "I feel so much better just saying my feelings aloud."

Tod and Jane agreed, "We do too—once we speak about our feelings, they aren't inside our head or heart anymore, which means we can let them go," Tod said. He was glad that they had decided to come to talk with Erick.

"Do you want to go exploring now?" Jane asked.

Erick nodded, "Yes! That would be great!"

No longer grumpy, Erick scrambled to his feet to show his friends some awesome things he found on his walk to the secret cave. Tod and Erick then showed Alice and Jane the other items they'd collected throughout their last few adventures.

They were very impressed.

Every item was on its own shelf in the cave. "This cave is special because it has many places to put our treasures," Erick said. The more he showed his friends their trove of goodies, the further away his grumpy mood seemed to be.

Erick felt very lucky to have such good friends. He also felt very happy that he learned something new about his emotions.

~ ~ ~

Learning to feel your emotions without letting them control you is an incredible gift you can give yourself. You cannot control how you feel, but it's important to understand why you feel a certain way. Talking about your emotions will help you move through them and give you a better understanding of yourself.

Baxley Gets the Job Done

Being there for your family is an important part of life, especially when they need you. Having your family's love, guidance, and strength are things that can give you an amazing power to know you can accomplish anything. Your family is there for you when you are happy, sad, angry, excited, good, or bad.

Wouldn't you be there for them in the same way?

Baxley is a young sparrow who lives in a magical forest where the bees have jobs and the rabbits run races. His family is a family of sparrows who work just as hard as they play. Each change of the season brings a new task for his family to tackle. When one member doesn't do their part of hard work and has too much fun, the entire family can suffer. Baxley learns a lesson about how hard you have to work to give your family a chance to thrive.

~ ~ ~

Winter in the forest would be ending soon. The icicles were melting, and the stream was beginning to drink in all the snow as it drained down the slopes and hills. Baxley and his family were flying back to their homeland, to warmer weather where they wouldn't have trouble finding food and playing games in sunnier weather.

Everyone in Baxley's family agreed that there was no place like the forest. The wind whispered tales of nature, battles, and triumphs. The water trickled songs of happiness and love. The leaves rustled gladly when the sparrow family returned.

And in spring, the entire forest burst forth with life.

All the animals came together to have great feasts, welcome new family members, and celebrate the coming of a new season of life.

This year, Baxley's older cousin Charles was in charge of getting the team together to build nests for the family to live in. The flock voted Charles to lead because he was the family's oldest nest-builder.

Baxley and a group of his family, including Charles, flew to the forest faster than the other members. When he saw the family's trees,

Baxley's happiness burst through his feathered chest and he twisted his wings, which made him fly into a double loop.

But his excitement wasn't long-lived. Baxley realized how much work they had to do. Their flock had grown so large that they needed fifty nests!

Charles never seemed to take his duties too seriously. He moved slowly, gathering supplies, and kept forgetting where he left the sticks, feathers, and soft bits that would cushion their nest.

Charles was more interested in having fun at night and sleeping through the day. He had a lot of energy that would make him a good leader, but it didn't seem that he was getting very far on planning.

Baxley was worried, but every time he talked with his cousin about it, Charles shrugged his wings and said, "We have lots of time, Cuz!" Cuz was a nickname that Charles called everyone, not just his cousins. Baxley would roll his eyes at this because instead of taking the time to call other sparrows by their names, Charles took the easy way out.

But Baxley knew that they did not have lots of time. Soon, the entire family would be coming to the woods, and they would have nowhere to live.

Baxley made a plan. He knew that he could not build fifty nests on his own, but he could collect items just in case Charles did not follow through on his duties.

While Charles played all night, Baxley gathered supplies during the day.

Baxley found one place to add all the items. He separated the berries, sticks, and leaves into piles.

Other sparrows in the nest-building group saw Baxley working hard and started to ask if they could help. Baxley was pleasantly surprised to find out that his fellow birds wanted to assist. It wasn't that Baxley thought the others were as useless as Charles. He knew that he wasn't the leader in nest building. He also hadn't asked any of them for support.

Baxley was touched that the other birds offered it anyway.

Baxley and his team worked in the rain, in the sunshine, in the warm weather, and in the cooler weather. When it was time to rest, they did so together at night. When it was time to eat, they all shared the berries they found.

Soon, he found that their supply piles were so large that they had to start building nests. When that happened, Baxley discovered that he was the sparrow that all the others on the team turned to. Once again, Charles was nowhere to be found.

Baxley separated the group in two.

One would start searching out trees where nests could be built, and the other would bring the supplies to these trees.

Then, they would all build the nests together.

Before Baxley knew it, they were at ten, twenty, thirty, then forty nests! He was so proud of his family and friends that he planned to have a party for them when they finished the last nest.

One day, when they had three nests to go, Charles flew into Baxley. Baxley could see that his cousin was panicking, so he asked, "What's going on, Charles?"

Charles fluttered back and forth, his eyes darted around, and he chirped, "They will be here soon! We don't have anything done! We've failed the flock! Everyone is going to know I did a terrible job!"

Baxley shook his head, "I agree you weren't there when we needed you. But we are almost done with the nests. I couldn't find you to tell you about it." Baxley waved his wing into the air to show Charles how they completed the nests.

Charles' eyes went wide in shock and then relief. He cawed loudly with excitement, "CUZ! That's amazing!" He said, "The flock is going to be okay!"

Other birds from the group flew down and stood next to Baxley. One girl sparrow named Jess stepped forward and said, "Yes. And it's all thanks to Baxley. He started doing things without being asked. He was a good leader. He got our team to get the nests done."

The other sparrows nodded in agreement. Baxley looked around at the rest of the team and said, "You guys all stepped up too! We worked very hard together, and now the flock will be taken care of!"

The crowd nodded in agreement.

Baxley turned around to an embarrassed-looking Charles. "I guess the flock picked the wrong bird to lead the team," Charles said, looking at the ground.

Baxley shook his head. "No, they believed in you. But you didn't believe in yourself, so you ran away. Next time you get voted to do something, even if you don't think you can do it, you should do it anyway. Then you can find pride in yourself."

Charles smiled, "Thanks, Baxley. I'm sorry I let you down. But I'm glad you were here. I will tell the flock you did an amazing job. If they or you put your trust in me again, I'll make sure not to let any of you down."

Baxley nodded at his cousin, happy that Charles had learned a lesson.

But Baxley was even happier and surprised at the amazing job they all did when they came together.

~ ~ ~

Being a leader and showing people through actions, not words, is an amazing way to inspire true friendship and change. Don't put off something difficult because you don't think you can do it or have a better time somewhere else. It pays off to work hard. You build pride in yourself and find that sacrifice, commitment, strength, and love will carry you through to help you accomplish incredible things.

The Mermaid Life

Have you ever wanted to try new things but realized how hard it was to do once you've started? What do you do when you find something that seems to be too hard for you? Do you stop doing it, or do you keep going? What happens when you make a mistake? Do you know how to learn from your mistakes, or do you think that you aren't cut out for a new thing when you make a mistake?

I'll tell you a secret—everyone makes mistakes. Mistakes are the way we learn how to do things!

Making mistakes is a great way to find new solutions and seek answers. Mistakes are great!

This story is all about mistakes that three mermaids make. They help one another out and learn new things. Do you think they reach their goals?

~ ~ ~

Winter, Petunia, and Angel were three mermaid friends. They could swim and play all day long. But they wanted to do more than just play. Each of them had a goal they hoped to reach.

Winter, who had black hair, blue eyes, and a blue tail to match, wanted to be the fastest mermaid in the village. She wanted to swim as fast as the ships that skimmed the water above.

Petunia had pink hair, and eyes the same green as seaweed. Her tail was pink, and it changed to blue when the light hit it right. She wanted to create the prettiest decorations for other mermaids. She would search the bottom of the ocean floor to make the fanciest decorations she could find.

Angel's hair was a lovely shade of purple. Her tale was the color green of the greenest gemstone. Angel loved sea creatures. She enjoyed examining them and finding new life in the sunken ships from pirates. Every time she explored, she was amazed by the different things she saw.

The three mermaid friends lived in a village deep within the ocean. The water was cool on their skin, but they were never cold. The town was surrounded by a tall wall of brown and green seaweed that swayed back and forth with the water's motion. Angel would say it looked like they were always dancing to slow music, Petunia would say that it looked like they were rocking in a chair, and Winter would say they looked like they were being pulled around by invisible strings.

The mermaids always had a lot of fun talking and imagining things together.

On one particular day, after school, the girls went their separate ways to practice their goals by themselves. Winter was racing the ships on the surface, Petunia was looking for the best ocean trinkets, and Angel was beginning to look for new ships she hadn't explored yet.

Winter couldn't seem to keep up with the ships. She kept getting lost in their wake and foam they put off.

Petunia couldn't find the right trinkets for her decorations. Everything she saw was broken or smashed

Angel couldn't find anything new to study. She looked around the sunken ships and talked to little crayfish who shrugged their shoulders, shook their heads, and told her to "go look someplace else."

Disappointed, the mermaids came back together and discussed what their problems were.

After realizing they all had had a hard day, Petunia got an idea.

She popped her head up and said, "What if we helped each other?"

A smile spread across Angel's face as Winter's head bobbed up and down in excitement.

Winter said, "That's a great idea!"

Angel said, "I'm in!" Then, Angel paused and said, "But how will we help each other?"

The girls placed their head in their hands and thought for a few moments.

"I got it!" Winter said, "Each day, one of us will do our thing, and the other two of us can help them. After three days, each of us will have practiced."

The other two mermaids shook their heads "yes," in agreement. Petunia clapped her hands, and Angel jumped up to do a flip in the water.

"How exciting," Angel said. She was happy to have her friends while working on reaching her goal. "We'll meet you near the surface tomorrow, Winter. We can race the ships with you first. Then, we can search for trinkets with you the day after that, Petunia." Then, on the third day, Angel would explore deeper, darker places and wouldn't have to worry about getting scared, which sometimes happened because the sunken ships were really deep and really dark.

The next day, the three mermaids met close to the surface. There was a canal where ships sailed through. They sailed one right after another, and if Winter reached the end before one ship did, she knew she was closer to reaching her goal. But, if the ship got to the end of the canal before she did, then Winter knew she would be able to go back and try again with another boat.

Winter explained her system to her friends, and they agreed to try it first before offering suggestions.

Petunia and Angel found out how fast Winter really was when they started. While she wasn't fast enough to outswim a boat along the whole canal, Petunia and Angel were quickly left in Winter's wake.

When her friends reached the end of the canal, Winter was waiting for them patiently. She had a confused look even though her friends hugged her and said, "That was amazing!" and "You're incredibly fast!"

"Thank you," Winter said, squinting up to the surface, "I think I need to get closer to the surface to avoid the wake from the ships."

Petunia and Angel gave each other a worried look.

"I don't know if that is such a good idea," Angel said, "you might get caught on one of their human tools."

Winter shook her head. "No, I think I'm fast enough to miss them all." She blinked her large eyes at her friends and asked, "Would you watch me just in case?"

Petunia nodded and said, "Yes, but just to let you know, we think this is a bad idea."

Winter smiled, "Don't worry. Everything will be okay."

But everything wasn't okay. Instead, Winter got caught in a net thrown into the water to catch fish. Petunia and Angel rushed to her and cut a hole in the net.

Winter slid through the gap, grabbed her friend's hands, and got pulled to safety. When they were far enough away from the ship, she hugged them tightly and said, "Thank you! I'm so sorry I didn't listen. I just thought if I could get close enough to the surface…"

Angel interrupted, "We are glad you are okay. That is the point. It was a good thing we were here to help."

Petunia added, "Yes. And, if you had done it when you were alone, you may have had a different outcome. Thankfully, now you know."

Winter ran a hand through her black hair and gave a nervous laugh, "Yes. I will never do that again. I'll just practice harder and exercise more. I know now that there are no shortcuts to hard work."

On the second day, Petunia and her friends went closer to the shore to pick up some sea shells. Sea shells could be green, blue, red, white, or more colors. Petunia loved to decorate with them. She knew she could make the prettiest designs with these and knew that the waves washed back and forth closer to the shore, and it was easier to find shells there.

Winter, Angel, and Petunia had small bags they would stick pretty things in, and they would dig through the sand with their hands or shovels made from seashells and coral. Petunia liked being close to the shore because she could feel the sun's warmth, and while she knew that she didn't want to ever get out of the water, the different temperatures made her happy.

The friends went in different directions while searching. Petunia went north, Winter went south, and Angel went to the west. They dug through the sand and collected the items they found the brightest color and those with unique shapes.

When Angel's bag was almost full, she turned around to tell her friends but could not see Petunia anywhere. "Winter!" She yelled, "Have you seen Petunia?"

Winter swam quickly over to Angel and said, "No. I thought she was with you!"

The mermaids swam back the way they came, calling and searching for Petunia the entire way. When they got to their starting place, they could feel the tide coming. Winter looked up and saw that the waves were washing over them. She said, "Oh no! Do you think she washed up onto the shore?"

Angel gave Winter a worried look and took off toward the surface. She poked her head out in time to find that Petunia was stuck on the beach.

She stuck her head back into the cool water and called down to Winter, "You're right, she is there! Let's help her!"

Winter and Angel moved quickly to build a long stick for Petunia to grab. Then, they swam as close as possible without getting sucked into the tide. They popped their heads above the surface and called to Petunia, "Grab on! Pull yourself to us!"

Petunia shouted back, "Okay!" She scooted herself toward the water's edge and watched the pole come closer to her. When it was in grabbing reach, she caught ahold of it and pulled herself to her friends as she bobbed over the waves.

When she got over to them, she breathed a sigh of relief, "Thank you. That was scary."

Winter remembered what happened to her yesterday and said, "I'm sure it was! Lucky we were here!"

Angel laughed nervously and said, "At least we know when the tide comes in now. Maybe we should wait until later or go earlier on a day that we don't have school?"

"That's a great idea," Petunia said. "I wouldn't want to get caught on the shore again. It was far too hot and dry up there.

As the mermaids swam home, they dug through the treasures they found, and Petunia got some great ideas for new designs. She couldn't wait to get started.

Angel led the group to her favorite exploring spot on the third day. She said, "Things get *really* dark, but there should be no places for us to get stuck in nets or sucked up onto the shore."

The friends gave each other a knowing look of relief.

"If you get scared, call out to me, and I'll come to you."

"Why don't we stay together?" Petunia said. "When we separate, it seems like we get into trouble."

Angel thought for a moment, then said, "True. Good thinking." She looked out along the sunken ships and pointed to one, "Let's go there. I haven't checked that one in a while."

And so, the friends swam over to the boat.

Years of being stuck at the bottom of the ocean had worn away the wooden beams that made up the body of the pirate ship. Large holes had formed in places where the mermaids and other sea life could swim through. Inside the boat, it was much darker, but the friends could see old items from the human world, like a cracked mirror that turned green because of how long it had been in the saltwater and a few similar shaped pieces that seemed to be from some kind of board game.

Petunia and Angel would stop every now and then to examine a new item they found. Winter wasn't quite as brave. She would look at the things they were looking at but didn't want to touch anything.

At one point, Angel went through a doorway. She yelled and hurried out of the room quickly. She grabbed ahold of her friends and pulled them out of the sunken ship, through the holes, and into lighter water.

"What was wrong?" Petunia asked. She was having a good time. She was getting ideas from seeing the different types of decorations humans had.

Angel rushed to Petunia's side. Winter, hearing Angel's yell, hurried back to her friends. She arrived just in time to hear Angel say, "I saw a fish with huge yellow eyes and enormous, sharp teeth! I think it wanted to eat me!"

"No, I don't." The mermaids jumped and whipped around to the voice.

The large fish smiled, its enormous teeth coming together in a crooked line.

"I don't eat mermaids. I eat seaweed!"

"Oh. I'm so sorry," Angel said. "I haven't seen a fish like you before. I was just startled. Can you tell me your name?"

"My name is Indigo. I am a sunken ship fish. I like the dark and staying in the shadows. The water is cooler down there. But I've seen you come around lately, so I wanted to say hello! I didn't want to scare you."

Angel smiled and was so relieved to meet Indigo that she said, "Thank you for saying hello to me. I'm so glad you did. Now I know that we have a new friend to look for when I'm exploring."

Petunia and Winter smiled and said, "We're happy to meet you too. We'll be happy to explore with you both too."

The mermaid friends all had success with their projects. They all had some mistakes and problems, but they now knew that if they worked together, they could accomplish anything. And with their new experiences, they each learned something about themselves and how to correct mistakes next time.

They all looked at each other and smiled, happy with their new friend, their lessons, and reaching a new level with their interests.

~ ~ ~

All three mermaids were working toward something they wanted above all else (besides friendship). They had problems and worked through them together. Instead of getting frustrated, they didn't give up even when they were scared. They knew it was okay to make mistakes because only when we make mistakes can we learn new things about ourselves.

Sidnee and Her Problem

Do you ever have a problem that you don't feel you can solve? Do you get embarrassed because it seems like it should be an easy fix or something you should know how to do? Do you have a hard time admitting that you are having issues?

We all have things that we have problems with. But when we talk about them with our parents or someone who cares about us, we can get help. Knowing that other people struggle with the same issue or something similar can help you let go of any awkward feelings.

~ ~ ~

Sidnee was a fairy who lived with her family and other fairies in a large, hollow tree. Their tree was called a colony. There were hundreds of homes, shops, parks, swimming spots, schools, and so much more within the tree. Each area was carved out of the wood in different nooks, crannies, and shapes. Homes in the hollow tree were larger than the shops where people searched for food.

Sidnee's family lived in a carved-out cubbyhole near the bottom of the tree. Sidnee's room was cozy. She had small lightning bugs that would light up her room when it was dark, and she had a little window that shone the light into her room during the day. Right in the middle of her room was part of the tree she could climb and play on. The tree even had a little nook in it where she could hide her most secret stuff. She slept on a pink bed with a dandelion tuft as her pillow. Green leaves covered her and kept her warm at night.

Sidnee was mostly a happy fairy.

However, she still hadn't learned how to use her wings when it came to flying. Flying was part of being a fairy; she just didn't understand how, even though she wanted to. She wanted to fly with her friends and family. She tried to fly on her own up the hollow tree stump to go to other levels and see what the rest of her colony had to offer.

But, every time she tried to flap her wings in flying class, her back muscles hurt, and her wing muscles wouldn't listen to her.

She was the only fairy in her class who hadn't started flying yet.

Every day, all the other fairies would line up, outside the tree, between the long blades of grass, and start flapping their wings. One fairy would fly above the grass, another would weave in and out of the grass strands, and others could do flips, fly together holding hands, or even shoot straight up into the sky.

Sidnee would just stand there, looking into the air, and try to will her wings to move. Sometimes only her left wing would move. Other times only her right wing would move, and once in a while, they would both move, but each would flap in different ways.

She would try to jump into the air and move her wings, she would try to stand still and try to take off, but nothing worked.

After a week of trying to fly and watching her classmates get better and better at it, Sidnee became very discouraged about her problem.

Instead of trying to fly, she plopped down onto the ground and hid her face behind her hands.

Miss Periwinkle, the flying teacher, came up to Sidnee and knelt next to her. Her long pink dress blew slightly in the breeze, and Sidnee noticed that she smelled like a rose.

"What is wrong, Sidnee?" Miss Periwinkle asked. She placed a comforting hand on her student's back.

"I can't fly. I'll never be able to fly. I'm a bad fairy." Her voice wavered with emotion, and Sidnee could feel her tears getting ready to spill over her cheeks.

"That is not true. Many fairies have a hard time their first week. Your muscles haven't built up yet, and your wings need time to learn to fly together."

Sidnee looked up at her teacher's kind face. "All the other students are flying just fine."

Miss Periwinkle gave Sidnee a soft smile and said, "You should not compare yourself to others. We are all at different places with different abilities that develop in our own time. You cannot match what someone else does because they are not you."

Sidnee sniffled a little and rubbed her eyes to stamp out her tears. What Miss Periwinkle said made sense, but it didn't make her feel better about not being able to fly. She really was just disappointed in her wings and wanted them to work correctly.

Miss Periwinkle said, "Tell you what . . . why don't you go home to practice over the weekend and see what the beginning of the week holds for you before you're too hard on yourself?"

Sidnee let out a long sigh, and she nodded her head. "That sounds okay," she mumbled. She then got up because the class was over. The other students were starting to land, and Miss

Periwinkle needed to give them her attention. She smiled at Sidnee one last time and said, "You will be amazing."

Sidnee wanted to believe her, but she just couldn't at the moment.

Soon after the students started to leave, Sidnee saw her dad waiting for her at the exit. She went to him and put her hand in his.

"What's wrong, kiddo? You look positively sad."

Sidnee shrugged. She wasn't ready to talk about her flying problems with anyone else yet.

She went to bed thinking about what her flying teacher said, and decided that she would practice flying by herself, in the morning.

The next day, bright and early, Sidnee left a note for her mom and dad. Then she walked out of her house and went straight to a meadow. It was so close to the break of day, the sun was just starting to shine, and the dew hadn't even dried from the flower petals and leaves yet.

Sidnee stood in a clearing, surrounded by purple daisies, and looked at the sky.

She clenched her fists and willed herself to hover off the ground.

Nothing happened.

Sidnee took a deep breath in and blew it out.

She scrunched her face up, tightened her fists, and jumped. Her wings did not move.

She opened her eyes and stomped her foot.

Her anger was starting to rise through her chest. She was getting mad at her wings and wanted to yell.

"Getting angry isn't going to help you." Sidnee started at the sound of her dad's voice.

"What are you doing here?" She asked her dad.

He smiled and said, "I knew something was wrong last night. When I heard you leave this morning and saw your note in the kitchen, I decided to see if you wanted my help.

"How do you know I am angry?" She asked.

"Because your face is red, and your fists are balled up. They look like they are ready to strike the air," he chuckled. "It's not the air's fault you're having problems."

Sidnee crossed her arms over her chest. "I don't think it's funny. I can't fly."

Sidnee's dad knelt to her, "You're right. It's not funny you can't fly. But getting angry isn't going to help you either."

"But nothing I do is working," Sidnee said. She threw her hands up into the air and groaned.

"That's because you keep doing the same thing." Her dad said, "I had the same problem. I was the last one who learned to fly in my class."

Sidnee looked at her dad in shock, "But you do amazing tricks and can fly so fast!"

"Yes. Now I do. But I am much, much older than you. I did not start out being an excellent flyer. I had to learn how my wings worked for my body. Just like I'm going to help you to do."

"Oh," Sidnee said, realizing she should have just talked to her dad yesterday. It probably would have helped her today. "What am I doing wrong?"

"Well, what do you keep doing that continues not to work?"

Sidnee shrugged. But, her dad said, "No. Think about it. What are you doing when you try to take off?"

Sidnee thought about it before she answered, "My wings won't move when I try to jump."

"Right. You're not putting any energy into your wings. You're trying to jump instead."

"Oh."

"Yes. When I walked over, I saw that you had tension in your face and fists. That tension needs to be directed toward your wings. Like when you are holding your breath? Instead, push that breath toward where your wings come out of."

"That makes sense!" Sidnee said as realization raced through her like lightning.

"Good!" Her dad stepped back and said, "Now try to fly."

Sidnee closed her eyes, but instead of scrunching up her face, she relaxed and focused her energy on where her wings connected on her back. She took a deep breath and then pushed the breath back to her wings.

After a few moments, both wings began to sway in and out.

Then they moved faster.

Then faster.

And faster still.

And when Sidnee opened her eyes, she saw that her feet were no longer touching the ground.

Sidnee was so surprised that her wings stopped working, and she started to fall to the ground.

She looked toward her dad and saw him smiling at her.

Instead of panicking, she focused her energy back on her wings and caught herself right before hitting the ground.

"Great job, Sidnee!" Her dad shouted.

And Sidnee smiled back at him.

Then, she flew into the sky around the stems of the flowers. She flew back to her dad and landed on the ground in front of him. "I flew!" She shouted and threw her arms around her dad's waist in a big bear hug.

"Yes! You did!'

"I'm sorry I didn't talk to you about my problem sooner. I wish I had, and you could have helped me!" Sidnee said, stepping back from her dad.

"It's okay," he said, "now you know you can count on me for anything."

And she did. She knew that even if she were nervous or embarrassed about a problem, she would go to her parents from that moment on. She was sure they would be able to help her.

~ ~ ~

Talk to your parents about your problems. Parental love is unconditional, no matter how big our failures are. When you talk to your parents about your problems, you'll find out that they have very good advice. Maybe, they've even gone through something similar to what you're going through.

Danielle and Daniel

Have you ever felt like someone wasn't listening to you? You try to talk, and they don't understand what you say, or they don't let you finish speaking? What happens when they interrupt you or misunderstand? Do you feel frustrated? Do you get angry? Do you yell?

Danielle and Daniel are twins who are also best friends. Although sometimes they don't listen to each other very well. When they feel as though the other isn't listening, they grow angry and frustrated, making it even harder to understand one another.

To find out what happens, continue with the story and see if they ever figure out how to stop fighting and start listening.

~ ~ ~

Danielle and Daniel live on a pirate ship.

Their dad is the chef and their mom is the captain. They have grown up on the same ship their entire life. They were even born on it! They loved living a pirate life. They got to travel to places all over the world and see amazing things. (Daniel even said he saw three mermaids once, but Danielle wasn't so sure.)

Their ship was the fastest of all the other pirate ships in the region, and their parents took cargo to places where the land was made out of green gems and others where the sky had cities in it. They saw floating boats, talking animals, fairies with a cast on their wing, and more. They loved adventure and always played a great game on their way to the next port to see what they would see next.

Danielle, who liked to be called "Dani," would always guess that they would see a fish wearing a suit and glasses.

Daniel would roll his eyes and say, "You always come up with that. You should try to be more creative!"

Dani would say, "If I stick with one thing, I have to be right about it!"

They would laugh together and talk until they fell asleep.

One particular night was very rough on the water. Their ship had tossed and turned all night due to a very big storm. Neither Dani nor Daniel got very good sleep.

In the morning, Dani brushed the sleep away from her eyes and swung her legs over the side of her bed. Daniel was in the middle of climbing down from his top bunk when he stepped on Dani's hand.

She yelped, "Ow! Daniel, you stepped on my hand."

Daniel grumbled, "I'm sorry, Dani. I didn't sleep well last night and didn't see where you were." He smoothed his hand over his messy hair and stretched into a big yawn. Although he didn't feel like getting up for the day, he knew that everyone else on the ship would have slept poorly, too, and he wouldn't be allowed to skip out on his chores.

Dani got up and rubbed her hand. It still hurt. But she was too cranky to say something. Instead, she walked over to get her clothes for the day and bumped into her brother. "Hey," Daniel said, "I said I was sorry, no need to bump into me."

Dani looked at Daniel, "It was an accident. I didn't sleep well either."

Both brother and sister looked each other over quickly and took a step back. They knew if they kept going the way they were, today would not be a good day.

After the twins got dressed, they left to eat breakfast and start their chores. When they got up on deck, they were shocked to see the mast had splintered in two. There were two groups of sailors on either side of the long wooden pole trying to move it so they could readjust.

Dani went over to her mom, who was at the head of the mast. She asked, "What can I do to help?"

Dani's mom shook her head, and her red curls rustled over her captain's jacket, "Nothing, right now. Although, we'll need you and Daniel later. Go eat breakfast and come back when you're done. We'll need you to clean up all the splinters and smaller pieces of wood.

Dani hugged her mom. She had seen some crazy stuff while sailing on a ship, but it hadn't ever broken because of the weather.

Daniel was already getting his breakfast when Dani came up to him. She said, "Mom wants us to meet them after we eat. We have to do some work with the mast."

Daniel rolled his eyes, clearly, still in a bad mood. "Fine," he said reluctantly.

Dani shook her finger at her brother, "You should probably . . ."

"Don't shake your finger at me," snapped Daniel.

"You don't even know what I was going . . ."

"I don't need to know. It wasn't going to be good," Daniel said, and he huffed away.

Anger ballooned in Dani's chest as she watched her brother walk off to sit with their dad. She clenched her teeth and scrunched up her face. When she whirled around to walk toward their table, then plunked down on the bench next to her dad and said, "You should listen to me. That was rude."

Daniel shrugged his shoulders and chewed his food. He didn't look at his sister, but that made her angrier. She wanted to know that he was listening to her, and she felt like he was being mean on purpose.

She pressed her lips together and shot dirty looks at her brother while he ate. Her father looked between his son and daughter and recognized they were a bit angry with each other today, but he wanted to see if they would work it out first.

After they cleared their plates, Dani and Daniel went to help the other pirates fix the boat.

The two groups had gotten the mast placed back onto the post. They were busy securing it into the straight and tall position. Daniel looked up to the top, "Do you think it's going to . . ."

Still mad at her brother, Dani snapped, "Fall over? I doubt it. The crew is very smart when it comes to fixing th. . ."

"That wasn't what I was going to say, Dani." Daniel stamped his foot and crossed his arms over his chest.

It was Dani's turn to shrug her shoulders and walk away. She found her mom, who motioned the twins to a point around the base of the mast. "Do you see that a bunch of wood broke off?"

The twins nodded.

"I need you to work together to clean it up. Then, I need you to sweep the mess into a pile while the other holds the dustpan. It's all very simple."

Daniel looked up at his mom and asked, "Will the mast . . ."

"He thinks the mast is going to fall," Dani interrupted. Their mom took a step back to see that her children were both in very bad moods. She smiled as she realized giving them a teamwork job to do might have been the best way to fix their differences.

"I don't!" Daniel said, "The mast is just a temporary fix, right, mom?" Daniel looked over at his sister and glared.

"Yes. We'll have to stop at the next island or port to get a new one. But for now, please clean everything up." She turned around, her boots clicking on the floor's deck as she went to see who else needed help.

Once their mom was out of earshot, he said, "What did you do that for? You don't even know what I was going to say."

Dani said, "I could guess, couldn't I? You did it to me. How do you like it?"

Daniel didn't like it at all but realized his sister was right. He ducked his head and blushed, embarrassed by how he treated his sister. "You're right. I'm sorry. I have been in a very bad mood since I woke up. I should have listened to you. I shouldn't have been rude."

Dani's irritation went away as she heard her brother's apology.

She realized that she, too, had started off her day in a bad mood and may not have handled her emotions as well as she could have, "I'm sorry too, Daniel."

They walked over to the broken wood pieces and started cleaning them up. By the time they had everything swept into a pile, brother and sister were friends again. They realized that even when people are cranky, that doesn't mean they should take things out on each other.

By dinner, the twins had completely shaken off their bad moods, and as they ate with their parents, they relayed the day with laughs, hugs, and love.

~ ~ ~

Sometimes teamwork can be the best way to work through issues. But, if you aren't willing to hear what the other person has to say, you won't be making a true effort. Listening is a vital skill to have when you want to treat people with respect, kindness, and gratefulness.

When you listen, even if you don't agree with the other person, you show them that you still care and let them know that what they have to say is important.

You should try to listen even when your mood isn't great—being generous means that you are thoughtful to others even when things don't go your way.

Vinny the Volcano

Do you ever get so mad you want to blow up? Does your voice get real loud? Do you feel like your angry emotions are taking over you? Has your throat ever hurt when you were done screaming because you screamed too hard? Do you feel embarrassed because you did something that you weren't supposed to do, or were you mean to someone who is always nice to you?

Feelings can get really big! Sometimes they are so big they feel like they could erupt out of us. But certain emotions can be harmful to yourself and others if you let them control you.

Vinny is a dragon. He gets so angry sometimes that he just bursts out with harsh words, and, every so often, with fire. The village he lives in has grown so used to his emotions that they call him Vinny the Volcano.

But Vinny doesn't like that nickname.

Not at all.

~ ~ ~

Vinny was a young dragon with green scales that faded to gold when the light hit them just right. His eyes were dark green like the trees in the forest. His mane was yellow like the sun.

His mother always thought he looked ready to burst into flames, even when he was sitting and playing by himself.

She would have been right because Vinny had a very bad temper.

Even though he didn't explode into a blaze of fire, he certainly got mad. When he got mad, he jumped around and shouted. He stomped his feet and threw things. He broke things. He would get so angry during certain times that smoke would come out of his nose, and flames would spark from his mouth.

There were even a few times when he set something on fire. When that happened, he felt bad about destroying something, and he would feel even worse because he continued to do the same thing almost every day.

Someone would say or do something to him and he would blow up like a volcano. He knew about volcanoes because they lived near one, and the other dragons in his village called him "Vinny the Volcano" every time they saw him.

This nickname didn't make him feel better.

In fact, every time he heard it, he felt worse about his inability to control his anger.

He was very embarrassed at how big his emotions were. But he didn't know what to do to help himself stop.

For three days, Vinny thought about how to stop himself from getting so mad. But when he couldn't think of an answer, he became even more frustrated with himself.

However, he didn't want anyone to see his big emotion release itself, so he walked out of the village as quietly as he could—even though he could feel the anger wanting him to stomp his feet—and went deep into the woods where he yelled, screamed, thrashed, and had a fit.

Although he was ashamed he blew up again, he was happy that no one was around to see it.

That was until he heard someone say, "Are you alright?" Heat rose into Vinny's cheeks because he had let a lot of anger out. He didn't realize anyone was around. He thought about running away without answering, but he was far too brave. Plus, if one more creature knew him like a volcano, he didn't think it would matter.

Vinny looked around to see where the voice was coming from.

He searched the trees and glanced over the sky.

He looked around the ground and behind his shoulder.

Finally, he looked to his left side and his right.

In a very small hole, in a very large tree, Vinny saw two tiny eyes blink at him.

"Was that you?" He asked the two blinking eyes.

"Yes. Are you alright?" the small eyes blinked again.

"Yes. I just got angry and didn't want anyone to see it. But I guess you did. So my plan didn't work."

"I did. Why didn't you want anyone to see how you're feeling?" The little voice moved closer to him. "You looked like you were in some pain."

"I was. I was angry."

"Oh." The small voice said, "I've been angry before. It feels just like how you showed it."

Vinny blushed again and put his head down, "Yes. But dragons aren't supposed to act that way. I've burnt things down, broken things, and once I hurt myself."

The little eyes blinked and stepped into the light. Vinny could see it was a little owl with brown feathers. "There are always things in the world that might make you angry."

"Yes, I know. But I'd like to be angry without erupting like a volcano."

The little owl closed his eyes and started to chuckle.

Vinny got embarrassed and started to walk away. He would have to find another place where he could think of how to stop getting so angry and blowing up so fiercely.

"Wait! Come back! I want to help you."

Vinny looked over his shoulder and said, "What do you mean?" He didn't realize that someone else would want to help him.

"I want to help you. I know what it's like to have big emotions. I used to cry all the time and cry very easily over little things. Is that how it feels for you with your anger?"

Vinny nodded, "Yes. I try not to get angry, but I cannot help it."

"Then, let's work together to fix it," the owl said.

"That sounds great. I can come back tomorrow if you're available."

"I am. I'll see you here!"

"Awesome. Have a nice day!"

Vinny went home happier than he had been in a long time. He didn't even think about being angry when someone yelled at him, "Hey, Volcano! How was your day?" In fact, he nodded at the other dragon and kept running home.

When he got into the house, he saw his mom making snacks for the family. Excitement twitched from his tale to his nose, and he went to tell her about his news but then stopped as a uneasy thought entered his brain. What if he told his mom he would fix his volcanic emotions but then couldn't? The idea made him a little scared. Quickly, he decided to keep his practice a secret, just in case.

Instead, Vinny stepped up to the counter next to his mom and said, "Would you like help to make snacks?"

Vinny's mom smiled and said, "Yes. That would be lovely."

Over the next few days, Vinny and the little owl, whose name was Mel, practiced keeping his anger from blowing up.

Mel would do and say all kinds of things to make Vinny mad. And Vinny tried not to explode.

Sometimes it worked.

Other times it didn't.

Mel decided that getting Vinny mad wouldn't be the only thing they should train on. Mel realized that Vinny was good at getting angry but maybe not so good at understanding WHY he got so mad so quickly.

This thought made Mel decide that when Vinny was angry, he should talk about his feelings instead of trying not to get mad.

When Vinny came to meet Mel the next day, the little owl said, "Instead of making you angry, I want you to remember when you blew up and talk to me about it."

Vinny agreed. He was willing to try anything that could help him conquer his anger problem.

Mel and Vinny sat on tufts of grass on the forest floor. They listened to the woods for a few moments, and Mel asked Vinny to relay a memory of when Vinny got angry.

"It doesn't matter what the memory was. Just think about how angry you were."

Vinny closed his eyes and thought for a few moments. One time especially came to mind. Someone in his school broke a homework project Vinny had done. He had made the model of a castle and set it down for one moment, and then the other student stepped on it.

Vinny knew that it wasn't really the student's fault, but he got so mad that day that he got sent home from school. Vinny opened his eyes.

"A classmate broke my castle. I got very mad."

"Why were you mad about it? Did the classmate do it on purpose?" Mel blinked his eyes.

"No, it was a mistake," Vinny thought. He got a little pang of sadness when he remembered seeing the castle in pieces. He blinked some tears away when he remembered, "I was really angry at myself. I was the one who put the model on the floor. I should have never done that."

"Ah," Mel said. "Do you see now that your anger covers up your emotions instead?"

Vinny tilted his head. "Wow. Yes. I guess so."

"So next time you get mad, you can take a step back and ask yourself what are you really feeling? Maybe that will help you not erupt like a volcano?"

Vinny smiled and said, "That's a great idea! Thank you, Mel!"

The next time Vinny got angry, he thought about why he was really mad instead of blowing up with anger. And he didn't blow his top.

The other dragons in the village soon stopped calling him "Volcano" and instead just called him "Vinny."

~ ~ ~

Emotions come in all shapes and sizes. Sometimes our happiness is bigger than our sadness, and sometimes our anger overtakes everything. What's important is to take a step back and think about why you feel the emotion you do. As you grow up, your feelings won't disappear, but when you learn more about yourself and why you feel the way you do, you'll begin to know yourself really well, which is awesome because knowing yourself will make you feel better.

Little Joe the Elf Wants to Be a Wizard

Have you ever wanted to try something but didn't think you could because of who you are? Well, it doesn't matter who or what you are. If you have a dream, you can do it. You just have to find the right way to accomplish your goals.

~ ~ ~

Joe is an elf who lives with his elf family in the forest. Because they are all elves, they spend their days frolicking, eating, running, and playing. But, Joe the Elf wants to do more. He wants to help all living things.

Joe doesn't just want to help all living things, he wants to do it with magic.

In the middle of the forest, down Cobblestone Lane, and right between the green trees are gates to a magic school. Joe the Elf has come across that school many times.

The first time he found the school by accident.

He was amazed, shocked, and inspired by what he saw through the wrought iron gates.

He saw a class outside, with all sorts of magical tools, floating candles, cauldrons, magic potions, a staff, and more. Creatures floating feathers, disappearing into nothing but glitter and flowers, and then they would reappear in a different place. Others looked like they were breathing fire, but it would turn into the water before it hit anything and caused any damage.

Joe blinked.

A warm feeling stirred in his belly and rose to his chest. His heart was golden and lighter than it ever had before. After a few moments, he left the school and just knew he had to go there.

It wasn't that he didn't have friends at his current school.

He liked the people and the school very much, but his school didn't do magic.

He knew that if he could do magic, he could help out all the living things he wanted to help out so much better.

He couldn't wait to tell his family.

But when he got home, his parents were making dinner, and his sisters were doing their homework. Nerves started to rumble in his belly, and worry pricked in his chest. Instead of saying anything, he hurried to his bedroom and closed the door.

Joe realized he was worried.

He didn't want to be worried, so he sat at his desk and thought about how to tell his family.

Joe knew that he thought best while he was journaling. Writing down his thoughts always helped him see what was troubling him.

He sat down and wrote about how he was worried his family would make fun of him.

He was worried that he wouldn't do well at school.

He was worried that his family would tell him he couldn't do magic.

Then, he thought about his family and realized how much his family loved him, and he thought about how they never discouraged him from doing something he had wanted to do before.

Joe decided to wait a few days to see how he felt.

While he waited for his nerves to calm down a little, Joe wandered by the magic school every day.

The path to the school was not on his way to or from his home, so Joe always made sure that he left for his activities with about an hour to spare. Even though he couldn't see inside the school, there was plenty of magic happening in the schoolyard.

Anytime he was there, someone was floating, disappearing, firing, sparkling, and engaging in other incredible things.

Every day, Joe got more excited to do magic.

Every day, he almost told his family.

One night after dinner, Joe went up to his room and tried writing down his thoughts. Only this time, he realized that even though he was nervous, he wouldn't be able to change his mind about magic.

He wanted to go to magic school.

He was nervous because he cared so much about it.

Then, he asked himself a question he hadn't thought of before. "What am I afraid of? What is the worst thing that my family would say?"

Joe realized they would never stop loving him.

Instead, the worst thing they might say to him is that he shouldn't go, but that didn't mean he had to listen to them (except for his parents, his parents made the rules). With a deep breath, Joe inhaled and stood. He marched back downstairs to the kitchen where everyone was getting ready to play a game, and announced, "I want to go to magic school."

His family stopped what they were doing and turned to look at him.

For a moment, no one said a word.

It was a long moment for Joe.

At one point, he could hear the ants marching overhead.

When he swallowed nervously because no one was saying anything, he almost thought he could hear his heartbeat. Then, he let a long breath out. Joe remembered that his family loved him.

As he exhaled, he saw a big smile break across his mother's face and his dad clapped his hooves together.

"That is great, son," his dad said.

"How can we help?" his mom asked.

"Where is the magic school?" His sisters asked and jumped up.

As he looked at all his family member's smiling faces, an amazing sense of love washed over him, and Joe couldn't believe he had waited so long to tell them. And he couldn't wait to go to magic school.

~ ~ ~

When you dream about something, try to do everything to make it happen. You are incredible and should never give up. Have passion and courage, and talk with the people who love you the most. They will support and guide you in any way to make sure you do what you were born to do.

Liam Wants an Adventure

There are millions of creatures in a magical land, big and small, short and tall, round and square, and many other shapes, sizes, and colors that might not even have a name. Think about the world you live in. Does everyone and everything look like you?

What do you think about when you come across something or someone different from what you've seen? Do you want to know more about it? Would you like to get to know them better?

Learning about something or someone by yourself is the best way to learn about things. When you research, investigate, and get to know something or someone, you have a different understanding of who or what they are.

~ ~ ~

Liam is a young boy who lives on the outskirts of a large village in a forest where trees grow in shades of red and the grass is the color of straw. One tall wall encircled Liam's town. No one that anyone could remember had ever gone outside the wall, and no one had ever come in either. The villagers were afraid to go outside the wall because they didn't know what was on the other side.

But the villagers were also very smart. They made everything they needed, and if they didn't know how to make something, they would work together to find a way to create it.

If someone needed paint, they had a villager who made the paint.

If they wanted to eat a new recipe, they would go to the best cook in town.

If they needed a tool for building a shed, they would go to the tool shop.

Anything they wanted, they'd find a way to make it—without leaving the safety of the wall.

Mostly everyone was happy that way because they were safe.

But not Liam.

It wasn't that he was unhappy in his village. He just thought that there could be more than just the village he lived in. Liam was a very creative boy and hoped to be an explorer one day. He was always caught daydreaming, and when he asked his parents, aunts, uncles, brothers, sisters, teachers, and others about what was beyond the wall, he never got an answer.

Instead, they would respond, saying, "Shhhh, we don't talk about those things."

"There are dangers outside the wall."

"Odd creatures live out in the world. We should stay away from them."

None of these responses appeased Liam.

He would continue to ask questions like, "Why don't we talk about those things?" "What kind of dangers are there?" and "Have you seen the odd creatures? What do they look like?" Most of the time, people would give him a grumpy huff and walk away from him. Some of the time, people would shrug their shoulders, shake their heads and tell him, "Liam—you should just listen. Your questions are unhelpful. We are safe. That is all you need to know."

But that wasn't all Liam wanted to know.

When no one was looking, he would sneak away to a tiny hole in the wall on the other side of his village, and he would look into the hole. He saw the red trees and golden grass there, and his heart grew full of excitement.

After he found a way to see the outside world, he would go at least once a week to see if anything changed. Each time he went, he found something new to look at. Once, there was an animal with blue wings and a beak. He knew this animal was called a bird because they flew over his village often. Then, he saw a tiny creature with green skin, black eyes, and wild blue hair that looked like cotton candy. Another time, he saw a small man with a pointed hat and a long beard who was picking berries.

Each time he went back, his imagination grew and ballooned so much that he couldn't keep his ideas in his head anymore. Then, he started writing.

He dreamed up thoughts and adventures he could go on if only he were allowed out of the gated door. Some nights he would stay awake from thinking about what he would need to take. Other nights his sleep was filled with dreams of golden grass and small creatures wandering through it.

One night, when he couldn't sleep, he crept downstairs to get something warm to drink. Warm drinks like tea always helped him drift off. But he saw that his grandfather was still awake and sitting by the fire.

Liam went over and stood next to his grandpa.

"Do you want a snack?" Liam asked.

"Sure. Let's get some hot apple pie from grandma," his grandfather responded.

"That sounds great." Liam smiled at his grandfather. Although he was much older, he never told Liam to stop thinking about outside or discouraged his ideas. Instead, his grandfather encouraged Liam to use his imagination.

Liam liked that very much.

While they were at the table, they blew the steam from their hot pie and placed once scoop each of vanilla ice cream on top, Liam decided to ask his grandad a question.

"Will you help me go through the outside gate?" He asked.

Liam saw his grandfather's eyes go wide and his bushy white eyebrows rise higher than he ever knew possible. His grandpa's blue eyes brightened up, and his lips widened into a warm smile.

"Is that something you really want to do?"

"Yes."

"You know you will cause quite a ruckus here if people find out."

Liam paused. He knew his grandfather was right. If anyone knew he had left the village, they might get very nervous or frightened for him and themselves.

"I think we should make it a secret then."

"Oh, I don't think we should make it a secret. I think you should talk to the town and give them your perspective. Then you can get permission and won't have to break any rules."

Liam thought his grandfather had a good idea, but if he couldn't convince the people at the meeting, his chances of leaving might forever be gone. However, he didn't feel comfortable breaking the rules either.

Liam nodded and said, "Will you help me prepare?"

His grandfather placed his hand on Liam's arm and said, "I think that is a great idea."

While it was hard for Liam to wait until the next village meeting, he kept himself busy by preparing all the reasons why he should be allowed to leave. His grandfather helped.

A few weeks later, Liam walked into the meeting with his grandfather and the rest of his family. He immediately grew nervous at having to speak in front of all the people, especially about going outside of the wall.

None of the people were supposed to talk about that.

He was going to speak to the entire town, his stomach was tied up in knots, and his chest seemed as though someone with a big fist was squeezing it. He was very nervous.

But Liam looked up to his grandfather, who had a sparkle in his eye and a kind smile. Liam knew that it meant his grandpa was rooting for him.

During the weeks before the town meeting, Liam gathered information, and he looked for signs that there was danger outside the walls. Surprisingly, besides a few old stories passed down from elders to the younger generations, there were none, and even those stories weren't too scary.

Liam wasn't sure where the fear of the outside came from, but he was hoping that the facts he found would help him get out into the world.

He did not let his nerves stop him. Instead, he took that energy and walked up to the stand when the village council called his name. He placed his speech in front of him and his hands on the edge of the tabletop.

Instantly, Liam realized he was clenching the hardwood in his hands, and while he could not relax them, he looked over the crowd until his gaze rested on his grandfather, who gave him an encouraging thumbs-up.

Liam nodded. He closed his eyes, took a deep breath, and let it out. As soon as the nerves were out of his chest along with his breath, he opened his eyes and began talking about how he longed for an adventure, and while he loved the village and the people in it, that no one should be forced to stay inside the wall if they didn't want to.

"There is a big world out there. I want to see it. I don't want to go away forever, but I also don't want to live my life knowing that I could have made a difference but didn't try. Adventures might not be for everyone, but exploring what is beyond the walls is right for me."

He continued, "I would never want to bring danger to the people of the village. But, after looking through our history, I can tell you that as far back as I have found, there is nothing outside the wall that has hurt anyone for 100 years or longer."

Liam could feel the room swell with support and emotion even as he continued to speak. He could feel his own emotions rising inside of him. He put all of it into his speech.

"It's time we break out and see what is beyond the wall. It's time we trust ourselves to take care of our community in bigger ways. It's time we try something different."

As he finished his speech, many villagers, including his family and grandpa, stood and clapped.

Liam was very proud of himself.

After he was done talking, the town council took a break away from the rest of the people. They went into a private room where they would talk about the events of the night and the decisions they would make.

People gathered around Liam, some of them were excited about going out of the wall, and others just wanted to tell him how good of a speaker he was. Liam was surprised to find out how many people felt the same way as he had.

Hearing that made him even more proud that he had done the hard work and spoke up for himself.

Soon after the crowd calmed down, the council came out and sat at their table. The head of the council stood to read off their decision.

Liam crossed his fingers and squinched up his eyes. He realized he was holding his breath too. He was so nervous about the outcome.

"In the matter of Liam's wishes to open the door, we grant that the gates be open from sunup to sundown. But they will remain locked overnight. Along with anyone else who would choose to, Liam can leave the town from here on out."

The town cheered, Liam's family scooped him up in a big hug, and tears formed in Liam's eyes. He was so happy that he had spoken with his grandpa. He might not have had the courage to take the steps without him.

"Thank you for your help!" Liam said as he hugged his grandfather tightly.

"You're welcome, and I can't wait to hear about what you discover first."

And neither could Liam.

~ ~ ~

Just because everyone has a specific idea about what could happen doesn't mean that it will happen. With hard work and learning, you can find something incredible and go on your own amazing adventure.

Epilogue

I hope you've enjoyed these stories and found inspiration to take on new challenges in your life. You can do anything you want. It's time to tackle some new roles and embark on new adventures.

Although our stories have come to an end, remember that you are an amazing kid! Never give up trying to do what you love the most.

Bonuses
Our Gifts For You

Subscribe to our Newsletter and receive these free materials

Scan Me

www.specialartbooks.com/free-materials/

Stay Connected with Us

Instagram: @specialart_coloring

Facebook Group: Special Art - Kids Entertainment

Website: www.specialartbooks.com

Impressum

For questions, feedback, and suggestions:

support@specialartbooks.com

Nadia Ross, Special Art

www.specialartbooks.com

Cover Illustration realized by
Maria Francesca Perifano

Printed in Great Britain
by Amazon

5f47ce9d-0641-4614-8571-3b5975613539R01